THE
FIGHT
TO
Flourish
STUDY GUIDE

JENNIE LUSKO

W PUBLISHING GROUP

AN IMPRINT OF THOMAS NELSON

CONTENTS

A NOTE FROM JENNIE

Thank you so much for joining me in this Bible study. It was written for women who want to thrive yet feel often as though they are failing. If you are anything like me, you might get frustrated when life feels a lot more like fighting than flourishing. It's like you're trying to get somewhere while walking knee-deep in mud.

But there's good news for you. You're already there. You are right where you are supposed to be!

I'm serious. You have already arrived at your destination. I'm not going to spoil the coming teaching, but you're going to learn in the first session how we are each like a seed packet. The picture might represent lush dahlias or bright roses or succulent strawberries or a ripe watermelon, but there we are, a seed. We might be small and insignificant, but we are growing. Spiritually speaking, Jesus is the picture on our seed packet, and we are becoming more and more like Him every day.

When we make the decision to trust in Jesus, we live our lives from the finish line. We understand that He has come to earth, died, and rose from the dead so we can live an abundant life, a flourishing life. The goal of a flourishing life is not to be perfect. Nor is it about the bloom. It's to engage in the present, point others to Jesus, and keep fighting through the struggle. It's the very things we struggle with that actually cause us to flourish right where we are. It's not about where you are going as much as it's about who you are becoming on the way there. Even when it feels gut-wrenching.

In this teaching, I have the privilege of sharing about our daughter, Lenya. She died and went to heaven on December 20, 2012. She was only five. My worst day on earth was Lenya's best day in heaven. In the battle against grief, I was reminded that,

> "[My] future is bright and filled with a living hope that will never fade away" (Proverbs 23:18 TPT).

This was true in the absence of my little girl and it is still true in everyday life—while I fight to be kind, to serve, to give, to hope, to love, and be a better woman, wife, mother, daughter, sister, friend, and leader.

God has put inside you and me the capacity and ability to live the beautiful flourishing life He has called us to live. It looks different for each of us. We're all on our own journeys and fighting in our own ways.

True flourishing comes from embracing the difficulty of growth. And we can't do that in our own strength. We fight with the power of the Holy Spirit. We fight with Jesus in our corner. We fight with God fighting for us.

We're not fighting and flourishing without purpose. The apostle Paul wrote,

> "Therefore we do not lose heart. Even though our outward man is perishing, yet the inward man is being renewed day by day. For our light affliction, which is but for a moment, is working for us a far more exceeding and eternal weight of glory, while we do not look at the things which are seen, but at the things which are not seen. For the things which are seen are temporary, but the things which are not seen are eternal" (2 Corinthians 4:16–18).

There's more to this life. More than our scars or bruises or cut lips. Everything we do on earth has an eternal purpose. Just wait, there's more. But for now, let's get growing!

HOW TO USE
THIS GUIDE

You can work through this study guide in a group setting or on your own. It's also formatted to work in conjunction with Jennie's book, *The Fight to Flourish*, and the video teaching. If you haven't read the book or won't get a chance to watch the video segments, don't worry. There's plenty of content that will help you begin, today, to activate growth in your life.

This study guide is divided into six sessions that include:

* An overview introducing the message of the session
* A review of last week's session (sessions 2–6)
* A start-up segment that sets the stage for the video session and the discussion to follow
* Video session and notes
* A set of in-depth group discussion questions drawn from the Bible, the video, the book, and real-life matters
* A closing prayer
* Four days of personal study to be completed on your own time
* A prayer from Jennie for you

If you want to maximize your experience outside the small group, spend time in the Dig Deeper portion at the end of each session. This includes four days of assignments to reflect on what you've learned as well as what God has been speaking to you about.

Timing ::

The times listed indicate the actual time of the video segments and the suggested times of the other group segments to help facilitate the meeting. This takes into consideration whether your group meets for an hour or an hour and a half. Group leaders should keep track of time.

What You'll Need ::

Unless otherwise marked, all the Scripture references in this guide are offered in the *New King James Version* (NKJV). If you prefer a different version, have a Bible or Bible app handy to look up the verses in the translation of your choice. While not necessary, as space is provided in this guide, feel free to use a journal or digital device to jot down notes or anything that speaks to you. Finally, while you don't have to, you'll get the most out of this guide if you read it alongside Jennie's book *The Fight to Flourish*.

For the Group Leader ::

Unless indicated otherwise, read each segment and questions. Select volunteers to read the Scripture and content from *The Fight to Flourish* and to close the group in prayer.

THE FIGHT IN THE
Dark

Overview ::

When we get to heaven, we will be fully made in the image of Christ, perfect and without blemish or shame. But until then, we live imperfect lives in an imperfect world. But no matter how hard the fight or dark the night, we can still flourish in the struggle because we are in Jesus Christ and He is the light that has overcome the world.

Session Start-up ::

(5 minutes)

LEADER: Read aloud to group.

A seed is destined to grow. But it's not as simple as tossing a few apple seeds into dirt and expecting an apple tree to sprout within days. Seeds must germinate. Then they must be planted. And then, with the right soil, water, air, light, and temperature, they grow. They do what they were born to do. And they do more than just bloom, they grow.

It's easy to dismiss the growth process when we're focused on the flourishing part. Let's be real. Flourishing is more fun. It's gorgeous. It's our "after" picture. It's where we show off results, showcase our victory, and personify success. We get our degree. We run the marathon. Our dreams actualize. We get it right and stop feeling like we're always failing at something. The thing is, flourishing is not reserved only for our desired outcome. Flourishing is interwoven with growth, with struggle, with fighting. And doesn't life seem like that sometimes? A fight? A fight to be kind, a fight to do what's right, a fight to focus on what matters most, a fight to live with purpose, peace, and passion.

In 1 Timothy 6:12, Paul the apostle who wrote most of the New Testament, encouraged us to,

> "Fight the good fight of the faith. Take hold of the eternal life to which you were called when you made your good confession in the presence of many witnesses" (NIV).

While we receive the gift of salvation and are born again, it doesn't mean we live in this trouble-free dimension flush with sunshine, rainbows, and fairytales. Paul gives us the directive to fight. In other words, it's not going to be easy. We're going to get sweaty and tired. We might even sport a black eye or a cut lip. We are born to flourish, yes, but we need the fight in order to flourish.

This truth is not meant to dampen your parade of living your best life. Jesus is with us in the fight and in the darkness. We are not alone. We are not left battling it out in our human strength. We don't need epic ninja skills or superhero punches. We hope in the darkness because we have the light of Jesus in us. Light that shines in and cannot be overcome by the darkness. Light that cannot be dimmed or snuffed out. Light that gives and keeps giving light to each of us. And no matter what situation we find ourselves in, whether we're wallowing in disappointment, crushed by heartache, or seeing stars from one of life's sucker punches, we can allow the Light of the world to shine through us.

Talk About It ::

(5-10 minutes)

What value does darkness have in everyday life?

Watch the Video ::

(15 minutes)

VIDEO TEACHING NOTES

Watch the session 1 video. While viewing the video, use the outline and space below to record key ideas or any thoughts you want to remember.

♦ What does it mean/look like to flourish?

♦ The process we are going through right now is the destination God has for us.

* Psalm 92:12–15

> "The righteous shall flourish like a palm tree,
> He shall grow like a cedar in Lebanon.
> Those who are planted in the house of the LORD
> Shall flourish in the courts of our God.
> They shall still bear fruit in old age;
> They shall be fresh and flourishing,
> To declare that the LORD is upright;
> He is my rock, and there is no unrighteousness in Him."

* Our life right now is motivated by and caused by starting at the finish line.

* When we follow Jesus, God looks at us and sees His Son.

* In this fight to flourish, God created us for a very unique purpose and for us to walk in it.

* God desires us to grow and live an abundant, full-of-joy life.

• When you hurt and it's hard, know that God is right with you in the pain.

• Psalm 18:28–29

> "For you will light my lamp;
> The LORD my God will enlighten my darkness.
> For by You I can run against a troop,
> By my God I can leap over a wall."

Small Group Discussion ::

(30-40 minutes)

LEADER: Read aloud each numbered prompt. Select a volunteer to read the Scripture and content from *The Fight to Flourish* book.

1. Read Psalm 92:12–15:

    > "The righteous shall flourish like a palm tree,
    > He shall grow like a cedar in Lebanon.
    > Those who are planted in the house of the LORD
    > Shall flourish in the courts of our God.
    > They shall still bear fruit in old age;
    > They shall be fresh and flourishing,
    > To declare that the LORD is upright;"
    > He is my rock, and there is no unrighteousness in Him."

List aloud three attributes of a flourishing life found in this passage.

2. In the video teaching, Jennie talks about how our lives represent a seed packet. The picture on the packet shows what the seed inside will grow to look like. The seed itself looks insignificant, but it has great potential. When we look to Jesus, the author and finisher of our faith, we have the potential of being like Him, the picture on the seed packet of our lives.

   Describe an instance when you felt overwhelmed by failure, great or small, few or many. How does knowing that God doesn't look at us and see our flaws, but rather Jesus, encourage you?

3. Read John 16:33:

   "These things I have spoken to you, that in Me you may have peace. In the world you will have tribulation; but be of good cheer, I have overcome the world."

   How does this promise from Jesus encourage you to trust Him and not give up during tough times?

4. Share what has been the darkest time in your life. Name one or two ways you have experienced Jesus working in and through you during that time?

5. Read the following Scriptures:
    *   John 1:4–5:

        "In Him was life, and the life was the light of men. And the light shines in the darkness, and the darkness did not comprehend it."

    *   John 9:5:

        "As long as I am in the world, I am the light of the world."

    *   1 John 1:5–7:

        "This is the message which we have heard from Him and declare to you, that God is light and in Him is no darkness at all. If we say that we have fellowship with Him, and walk in darkness, we lie and do not practice the truth. But if we walk in the light as He is in the light, we have fellowship with one another, and the blood of Jesus Christ His Son cleanses us from all sin."

    Take turns naming something these Bible passages teach us about the source and importance of light.

6. Consider the concept of us reflecting the light of Jesus. How have you reflected the light of Jesus to others? Talk about a time when you were encouraged by someone who reflected the light of Jesus to you.

7. In the video teaching, Jennie talks about beauty being possible in a dark place, even in our struggles. Read Psalm 18:28–29:

> "For You will light my lamp;
> The LORD my God will enlighten my darkness.
> For by You I can run against a troop,
> By my God I can leap over a wall."

What has it looked like in your life to "run against a troop" or "leap over a wall" as a result of God shining a light in your darkness?

Wrap It Up ::

(5 minutes)

LEADER: Read the paragraph below and select a reader to close the group in prayer. She can use her own words or be guided by the ideas below:

Today we have learned that God shines the brightest in the darkness. We can flourish in the dark and in the fight because He is in and with us. And there's more. God can heal and use our pain to uncover brilliance in our lives and in those around us.

Let's close this session in prayer.

- Thank Him for being the light of the world.
- Ask Him to reveal opportunities in which you can shine for Him.
- Pray for strength, courage, and grit to do the hard things, the things you don't feel like doing.
- Ask your heavenly Father to use your pain or your darkest day to bring about good in the life of someone who needs it most.

Dig Deeper

Day 1

STUDY

Read and meditate on Romans 3:21–26 NIV:

> "But now apart from the law the righteousness of God has been made known, to which the Law and the Prophets testify. This righteousness is given through faith in Jesus Christ to all who believe. There is no difference between Jew and Gentile, for all have sinned and fall short of the glory of God, and all are justified freely by his grace through the redemption that came by Christ Jesus. God presented Christ as a sacrifice of atonement, through the shedding of his blood—to be received by faith. He did this to demonstrate his righteousness, because in his forbearance he had left the sins committed beforehand unpunished—he did it to demonstrate his righteousness at the present time, so as to be just and the one who justifies those who have faith in Jesus."

Some people get so stuck in religion and religious things that they miss the most important part of the Christian faith—Jesus, and His life, death, and resurrection. It's not about what we do or don't do; it's about Jesus and His righteousness. Always.

REFLECT

In *The Fight to Flourish*, page xix, Jennie writes:

"The Bible teaches us that when we surrender to Jesus, we are, in a moment, made righteous. We don't earn salvation; we believe and receive freely. We don't pay for it—not with money, not with the good things we do. It's purely a gift from the God who loves us. We're covered by the grace found only in Jesus through His death and resurrection. And in that moment of salvation, we're made like Christ. So when God looks at us, He sees Jesus. That doesn't seem possible to me, but it's the way God does it, and it's beautiful.

"But until we get to heaven, where we will truly be perfect like Jesus, we're still here, in these imperfect bodies and minds. We're in a period of sanctification. That's a fancy way of saying that, yes, we're already in Christ, and yes, we're also still in the process of becoming more like him—right now. We're living in the dash between the date of our birth and the date of our last breath on earth. That last breath will lead us to our first breath in heaven with Jesus. But we're not there yet.

"Does flourishing in this life seem out of reach? It often feels like that to me. . . . The great news, though, is that we are actually in the process of flourishing right now, whether we feel it or not."

How does it feel to know you are declared righteous when you make the decision to receive Jesus as your personal Savior and trust in Him? Name one way this takes the pressure off the need to get it all right all the time.

How does this truth give you the confidence to live your life, failures and all?

_____

_____

_____

Write down something in your life that you would like to see improve or an area in which you feel as though you are constantly failing. Maybe you want to let go of a bad habit or desire more patience to parent your child well.

_____

_____

_____

It can be easy to replay the moments where we've missed the mark or gotten stuck in the mistakes we seem to make over and over and over again. Staying in that space keeps us from growing.

If you're feeling this way, write out a prayer to God. Ask Him to forgive you for the times you messed up. Thank Him for the new mercies He freely gives you each day. Ask Him to pour into your weaknesses His strength and to step in with His grace when you fall short.

_____

_____

_____

_____

_____

_____

_____

Paul experienced firsthand the power of the grace of God. Paul knew it wasn't a free pass to do whatever we want to do. He wrote,

> "What then? Shall we sin because we are not under law but under grace? Certainly not!" (Romans 6:15).

While grace doesn't give us a license to sin, we are also not bound by condemnation. Read Romans 8:1–2:

> "There is therefore now no condemnation to those who are in Christ Jesus, who do not walk according to the flesh, but according to the Spirit. For the law of the Spirit of life in Christ Jesus has made me free from the law of sin and death."

You may be so discouraged with the progress (or lack thereof) in your life. But that's just impatience talking. Never forget the One who is in charge of the process. You may not be where you want to be but, thank goodness, you are not where you were! God is faithful. God is good. And God is working on you. He is trustworthy. He will complete the work He started. Until then, rest in the grace of what Jesus did for you on the cross.

Spend a few minutes reflecting on what grace means to you. How has your life been changed as a result? Has it become something you take for granted, or something you really haven't thought of in a while?

_____

_____

_____

Now, fill in the following blanks:

Grace is _____ .

Grace can _____ .

Grace will _____ .

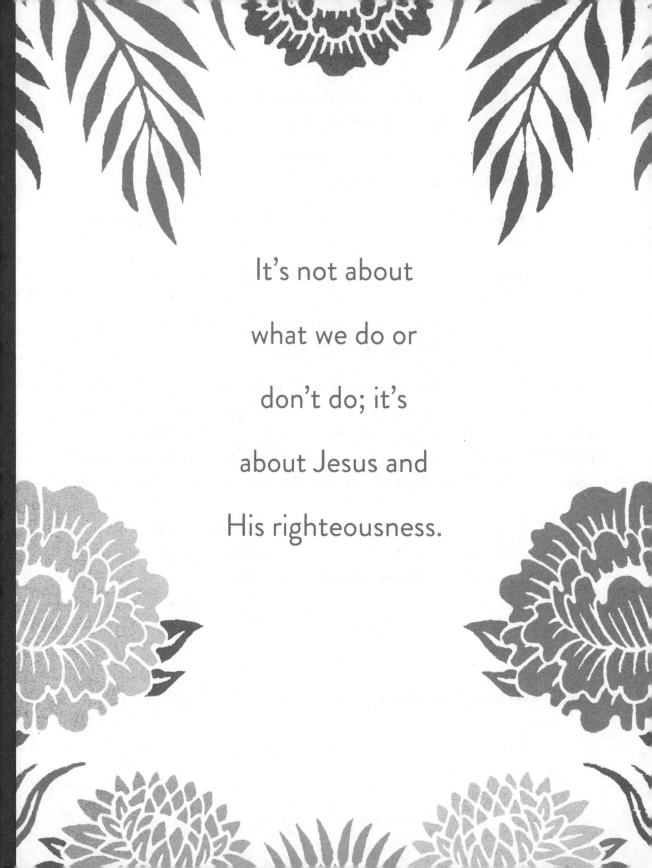

It's not about what we do or don't do; it's about Jesus and His righteousness.

Day 2

READ

If you are reading *The Fight to Flourish* in conjunction with this study guide, read chapters 1, 2, and 3 in the book.

REMEMBER

"You may feel as though you're not flourishing *because* of the fight, *because* of the struggle. But it's the embracing of the fight that will create the space to flourish. A fight for honor. A fight for a sweet spirit. A fight to choose to get uncomfortable. A fight to keep fighting. Jesus said,

"These things I have spoken to you, that in Me you may have peace. In the world you will have tribulation; but be of good cheer, I have overcome the world" (John 16:33).

Jesus doesn't mention overcoming the trouble; He tells us He has overcome the world. We want Him to take away the trial, but He's taking care of the even bigger picture: the world our trouble is in." (*The Fight to Flourish*, pages xx–xxi)

REFLECT

Jennie shares the tragic story of losing her five-year-old daughter Lenya. Journal a few paragraphs about your darkest moment and how you were able to see glimpses of God's love, comfort, peace, perhaps even joy in the midst of your pain.

Write down what you have learned, a breakthrough you experienced, or a shift in perspective from this video session or discussion. Prepare to share with the group next week.

REFLECT

God shines the

brightest in the

darkness.

Day 3

STUDY

No matter how hard things get, you can continue to grow. Most of us want to run from hard times. It's a space we'd rather not set foot in, let alone stay for a while and endure the pain, heartache, rejection, or disappointment. Read what the Bible teaches about how we are to view hard times.

> "My brethren, count it all joy when you fall into various trials, knowing that the testing of your faith produces patience. But let patience have its perfect work, that you may be perfect and complete, lacking nothing" (James 1:2–4).

Count it all joy? Sounds crazy, right? But the good news is that trials don't just show up to knock us down. There's a bigger plan at work. If we choose to let Him, God can use the hardship we face to help us become more and more like Jesus, to develop our character, and to give Him an opportunity to be our strength in weakness.

Think of a difficult time you went through. Write down three ways in which this situation changed you for the better. Maybe it's a truth you learned that brought to life a dormant faith or a character trait that grew in a way it wouldn't have without that difficulty.

_____

_____

Don't run from your trials. Don't shy away from surrendering to God because you're afraid of what may come. Be bold and courageous knowing you are safe in the arms of Jesus. Things happen that are beyond our control. Know as you walk with God, as you love and trust Him, that He won't allow you to be removed from His presence.

Read the following passage out loud:

> "Because he has set his love upon Me, therefore I will deliver him;
> I will set him on high, because he has known My name.
> He shall call upon Me, and I will answer him;
> I will be with him in trouble;
> I will deliver him and honor him.
> With long life I will satisfy him,
> And show him My salvation" (Psalm 91:14–16).

List three promises found in this Scripture. Memorize them and say them out loud when you feel overwhelmed. Keep them handy. Write them down in your journal, on a note posted on your mirror or in your phone, so you can refresh yourself with these promises when needed.

Promise 1 _____

Promise 2 _____

Promise 3 _____

REFLECT

A life that blooms with growth doesn't just happen. Progress requires effort and energy, stamina and sweat, persistence and perseverance. Think about what it takes for a plant to grow. After a seed is planted, it needs air and the right amount of water, light, space, time, and temperature to germinate and flourish. In other words, growth doesn't just happen overnight. The same can be said for us. We grow over time and—this is a big truth—we all don't grow at the same rate.

Reflect on what you were like a year ago. Since that time, journal the areas in which you have noticed growth. Where have you seen progress, no matter how slow? Note: This is not an exercise to unveil the full picture of what blooming looks like. None of us are going to find perfection this side of heaven. Be encouraged by even the small steps of forward movement you have taken in the right direction.

Now think back to five years ago. Journal your thoughts: have you changed for the better since then? Have some habits improved? Have you prioritized better?

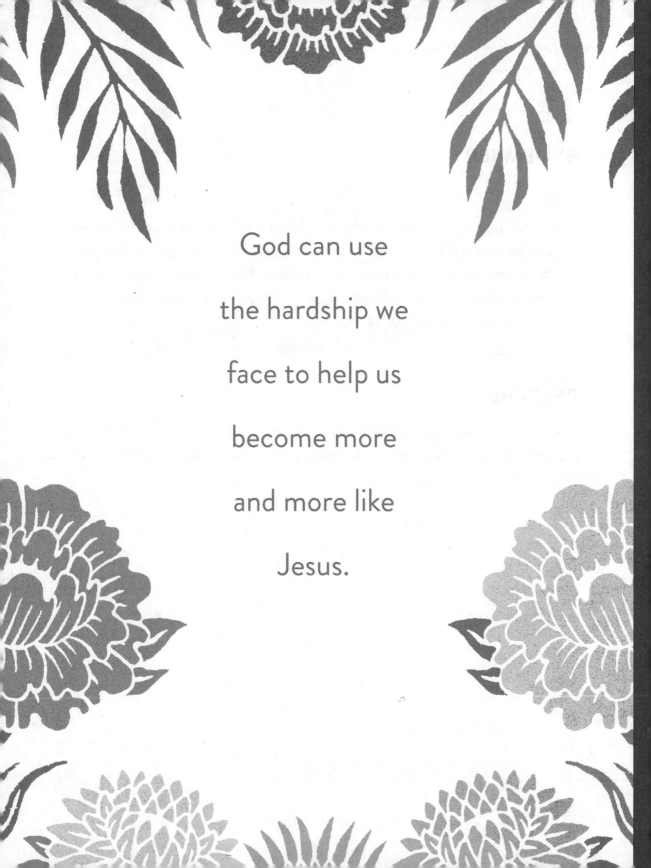

God can use

the hardship we

face to help us

become more

and more like

Jesus.

Day 4

REMEMBER

> "Everything we do in the current season is preparing us for the next one. We call this training for the trial we're not yet in. Fighting to grow sets us up to glow in the dark, so each step is essential to the next. The flourishing life is all about being faithful with the small things and watching God handle the impossible." (*The Fight to Flourish*, page 24)

PREPARE

If you are reading along in *The Fight to Flourish* book, read chapters 4, 5, and 6 this week. Capture any statements or phrases that motivated or challenged you and that you'd like to share with the group next week.

JENNIE'S PRAYER FOR YOU

Heavenly Father, I pray for this beautiful woman. Remind her that You are good, that You have designed her for this very moment, and that she can be the good thing You have created her to be. Give her boldness and strength to shine brilliantly in her world. Ignite in her a desire to flourish, wherever she is, and I pray she would know that even in the fight, she is flourishing. Nurture in her a readiness and a willingness for what you have in store for her life. In Jesus' name I pray, amen.

DON'T BLOOM WHERE YOU'RE

Planted

Overview ::

When we choose (and keep choosing) to grow, fighting forward and armed with God's strength, we can flourish wherever we are planted.

Review ::

(5-10 minutes)

Share one thing that stood out to you most from last session's video or discussion.

Session Start-up ::

(5 minutes)

LEADER: Read aloud to group.

When two boxers contend in the last rounds of a close match, there's a way to tell who is going to come out on top. The winner will probably be the one who put in their roadwork. In other words, if you want to come out stronger, you need to up your endurance game outside of the ring. The best way to do this is to hit the pavement running. Literally. Run long distances. Run intervals. Sprint. Intervals. This teaches us a practical faith lesson. When you do the spiritual roadwork, it's going to show in the ring of your life.

It's so much easier to coast, isn't it? To stay planted in our comfort zone of familiar and do what seems easiest rather than cultivate, with intention, the gardens of our inner lives. Maybe we've made habits of setting certain tasks or relationships above the higher calling of spending time with God. Maybe we often find ourselves distracted by social media or work or laundry. Or maybe we just go through the motions of being a Christian because, hey, it's better than not doing anything at all, right? But in order to flourish, we have to tend to our spirituality. No one can walk with God for you. No one can deepen your relationship with Him but you. Because when tough times creep your way—and they will—you're going to need His strength and wisdom and love to help you navigate through that treacherous terrain.

We fight forward every day by accepting responsibility for our spirits and positioning our dependence on God. While we don't have to work for our salvation, we work it out every day. Jesus performed the ultimate work for us by dying on the cross for our sins, but we are responsible to continue to fight forward every day in his strength. We win because we are in Jesus, but we still have to fight. And it's in this tension that we flourish.

One of the most effective practices to cultivate our spiritual gardens right where we are is to soak in Scripture. Don't just read the Bible; study it. Let the truths of God's Word sink deep into your spirit. Pray for understanding and revelation. Guard Scripture like a treasure. Memorize it. Need encouragement? Read Scripture aloud and remind yourself of the power that is found in what God says. Doing this can unleash a new perspective of where you are. So often we compare our growth process with someone else's or set unrealistic expectations for where we should be in life. Be encouraged, there is something beautiful happening right where you are!

Talk About It ::

(5-10 minutes)

How often do you have to fight against what you'd rather do instead of what you should do (the more healthy/productive/effective option)?

Session 2 Video ::

(12 minutes)

VIDEO TEACHING NOTES ::

Watch the session 2 video. While viewing the video, use the outline and space below to record key ideas or any thoughts you want to remember.

* Instead of focusing on the bloom, take a breath, look down, see where you're planted, and look up.

◆ Cultivate the ground you are planted in and water where it's hard.

◆ Keep your guard up.

◆ Proverbs 4:23:

> "Keep your heart with all diligence. For out of it, spring the issues of life."

◆ Your spirit is your responsibility.

◆ Ephesians 6:10:

> "Finally, my brethren, be strong in the Lord and in the power of His might."

◆ We're not called to carry the things that only God was meant to carry.

- Philippians 2:12:

  "Therefore, my beloved, as you have always obeyed, not as in my presence only, but now much more in my absence, work out your own salvation with fear and trembling."

- Sometimes we get easily distracted by all we need to do that we don't focus on our Savior.

- Story of Martha and Mary (Luke 10:38–42)

- It's important to study God's Word.

Small Group Discussion ::

(30-40 minutes)

LEADER: Read aloud each numbered prompt. Select a volunteer to read the Scripture and content from *The Fight to Flourish* book.

1. In the video teaching, Jennie mentions how we often focus on the bloom rather than what's happening inside us where we are planted. Jude 1:20–21 gives us sound instructions for how to flourish during the growth process.

   "But you, beloved, building yourselves up on your most holy faith, praying in the Holy Spirit, keep yourselves in the love of God, looking for the mercy of our Lord Jesus Christ unto eternal life."

   Discuss what it means to practice each of the following instructions:
   - Build yourself up on your most holy faith

   - Pray in the Holy Spirit

   - Keep yourself in the love of God

   - Look for the mercy of Jesus

2. We are responsible for our spirits. If we want to experience spiritual growth, we must make the choice to make it happen. At the same time, God, too, helps us grow when the pressures of life start to build.

   Name an obstacle that keeps you from tending to your spirit. What can you do, starting today, to prioritize your inner life over these challenges?

3. In the video teaching, Jennie shares an example of how she was walking around Disneyland for her daughter Alivia's thirteenth birthday. She wore a backpack full of diapers, wipes, snacks, and extra clothes for her son. By the end of the day, it felt like she was carrying dumbbells in the bag. When she opened it up later that day, she discovered her laptop was in there the whole time. Jennie had been carrying around unnecessary weight!

   Can you relate? Reflect on something that you struggle with letting go of. What keeps you from surrendering that weight to God? Paint a picture of what your life could look like if you allowed Him to carry it for you?

4. Share an experience in which you felt the unbearable weight of a challenge or trial and felt tempted to throw in the towel instead of trusting God. What did you do? What was the outcome?

5. In the video teaching, Jennie talked about the story of Martha and Mary in the Bible. Which woman do you resonate with and why?

6. In the video teaching, Jennie talks about the importance of studying Scripture. She says that storing up God's Word in our lives will fuel and empower us to spiritually keep our guard up. Name an instance where you have relied on what God says in the Bible to strengthen your spirit during a challenging time.

7. The psalmist wrote,

> "Your word I have hidden in my heart, that I might not sin against You" (Psalm 119:11).

What are some practical and creative ways we can hide Scripture in our hearts? Why do you think the psalmist connected having God's Word in our hearts to not sinning against Him?

Wrap It Up ::

(5 minutes)

LEADER: Read the paragraph below and select a reader to close the group in prayer. She can use her own words or be guided by the ideas below:

Today we have learned that we have to fight to grow and grow to fight and in all of these things, we are flourishing. We work. We rest. We fight. We pray. We serve. We sacrifice. We pour our hearts and souls into all we do, even the hard things, because that's what God has called us to. When we set our eyes on Jesus in each and every day, it sets the pace for a flourishing life.

Let's close this session in prayer.

- Thank God that His strength and His grace are sufficient for everything you go through or do.
- Pray for a renewal of joy and courage to boost your walk with Him.
- Ask your Father in heaven to develop in you an even greater desire to know Him and be known by Him.
- Ask God to help you become aware of and release the distractions that keep you from tending to your spirit.

Dig Deeper

PERSON STUDY / SESSION 2

⚡

Day 1

STUDY

Paul wrote a beautiful prayer to the church of Ephesus that reflected his desire for them:

> " . . .that He would grant you, according to the riches of His glory, to be strengthened with might through His Spirit in the inner man, that Christ may dwell in your hearts through faith; that you, being rooted and grounded in love, may be able to comprehend with all the saints what is the width and length and depth and height—to know the love of Christ which passes knowledge; that you may be filled with all the fullness of God" (Ephesians 3:16–19).

In this passage, we see some great spiritual goals for each of us to strive toward:

- that the Holy Spirit would strengthen us
- that Christ would dwell in our hearts through faith
- that we would be rooted and grounded in love
- that we would comprehend the depth of God's love
- that we would be filled with the fullness of God

Write out a prayer to God in which you tell Him your desire for these goals to come to pass in your life. Pray this every day and be open to the opportunities He will present to build and use these spiritual muscles.

_____

_____

_____

_____

_____

REFLECT

One of the most important rules of boxing is to keep your guard up. You do this by pushing your fists against your cheeks. Pretend you're holding two phones besides your ears. This posture can help us think about how we approach our spiritual life. Being a Christian is anything but passive. Yes, we rely on God for His grace, salvation, and strength. But we also work out our own spiritual growth. As Paul wrote,

> "Dear friends, you always followed my instructions when I was with you. And now that I am away, it is even more important. Work hard to show the results of your salvation, obeying God with deep reverence and fear" (Philippians 2:12 NLT).

On a scale of one to ten (1 being "not much" to 10 being "it plays a crucial role in my life"), how much of a priority do you place on the following spiritual practices:

Prayer

| 1 | 2 | 3 | 4 | 5 | 6 | 7 | 8 | 9 | 10 |

Listening to God/being quiet in His presence

| 1 | 2 | 3 | 4 | 5 | 6 | 7 | 8 | 9 | 10 |

Reading and studying the Bible

| 1 | 2 | 3 | 4 | 5 | 6 | 7 | 8 | 9 | 10 |

Memorizing Scripture

| 1 | 2 | 3 | 4 | 5 | 6 | 7 | 8 | 9 | 10 |

Worship

| 1 | 2 | 3 | 4 | 5 | 6 | 7 | 8 | 9 | 10 |

Fasting

| 1 | 2 | 3 | 4 | 5 | 6 | 7 | 8 | 9 | 10 |

As you reflect on your answers, list two practices you can focus on to deepen your spiritual growth. How can you make these two habits a priority?

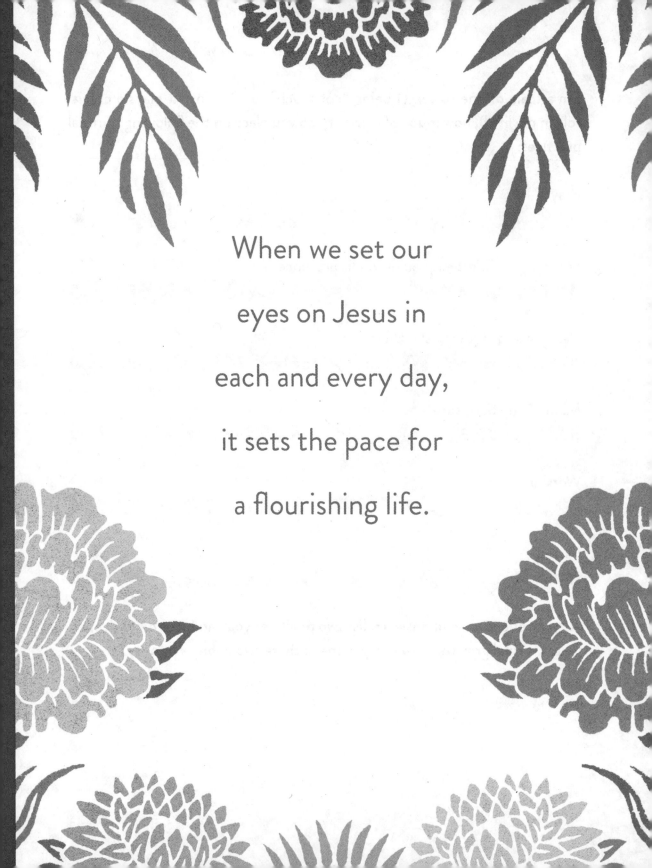

When we set our

eyes on Jesus in

each and every day,

it sets the pace for

a flourishing life.

Day 2

REVIEW

Review chapters 4, 5, and 6 in *The Fight to Flourish*.

REMEMBER

"We can delight in and commit our way to Him, and He will do the beautiful things that He wants to do in us and through us. We experience peace and confidence when we stick to the plan, even if it's one that God knows and we don't. This takes away the pressure of trying to figure it all out." (*The Fight to Flourish*, page 78)

REFLECT

When life doesn't make sense or we're not feeling the warm and fuzzies in our spiritual walk, it can be difficult to trust in God. Yet, when we do, no matter how we feel or what we are going through, He will not forsake us. Meditate on the following Scripture. Ask God to reinforce the truth of His trustworthiness in your heart today.

> "And those who know Your name will put their trust in You;
> For You, LORD, have not forsaken those who seek You" (Psalm 9:10).

> "Trust in the LORD forever,
> For in YAH, THE LORD, is everlasting strength" (Isaiah 26:4).

> "Blessed is the man who trusts in the LORD,
> And whose hope is the LORD.
> For he shall be like a tree planted by the waters,
> Which spreads out its roots by the river,

And will not fear when heat comes;
But its leaf will be green,
And will not be anxious in the year of drought,
Nor will cease from yielding fruit" (Jeremiah 17:7–8).

Write down any words or phrases that stick out to you.

_____

_____

_____

There is something

beautiful happening

right where you are!

Day 3

STUDY

Meditate on the following Scripture:

> "I say then: Walk in the Spirit, and you shall not fulfill the lust of the flesh. For the flesh lusts against the Spirit, and the Spirit against the flesh; and these are contrary to one another, so that you do not do the things that you wish. But if you are led by the Spirit, you are not under the law" (Galatians 5:16–18).

Let's get real for a moment about our need for the Holy Spirit. It can be so easy to become unglued. Some emotions feel so powerful, it seems impossible to pry ourselves out of their suffocating grip. We can't do this on our own. But the Holy Spirit produces in us self-control. He can do for us what we can't do for ourselves.

List two emotions that continually try to boss you around. Make a commitment whenever you start to get consumed by them to stop whatever you are doing, take a breath, and ask the Holy Spirit to step in and help you control them.

1. _____

2. _____

For the next forty-eight hours, keep track of when you experience these feelings. Write down how you kept the emotion in check (i.e., praying/taking a breath) and what the outcome was.

REFLECT

Emotions are natural. We are humans, after all, and part of the human experience involves our feelings. We get angry, sad, frustrated, disappointed—the list is long. But it's important to remember that feelings are not the boss of us. We may feel negative emotions, but we don't have to be controlled by them. And we don't have to allow them to fuel unhealthy responses. Self-awareness is the key to managing our emotions and keeping them in check. This is especially important when we get frustrated or disappointed when the picture on the seed packet doesn't quite match where we are in life.

> Think about the past twenty-four hours. Make a list of all the emotions you experienced (i.e., frustrated, happy, shocked, insecure, excited). Don't think too much about this exercise; just write what comes to your mind.
>
> _____
>
> _____
>
> _____
>
> Now, take three emotions that had a positive effect and write down a response or action that was fueled by that emotion. For instance, "refreshed"—"I woke up feeling great and decided to run for thirty minutes before work today."
>
> a. _____
>
> b. _____
>
> c. _____
>
> List three emotions that had a negative effect and write down a response or action that was fueled by that emotion. For instance, "annoyed"—"I was annoyed that I stepped on twenty Legos this morning because the kids didn't put them away last night. I gave them a piece of my mind when they woke up."
>
> a. _____
>
> b. _____
>
> c. _____

Think about the responses you listed above. When we allow our emotions to rule over us, chances are, we're going to do something we'll regret. This is why Paul wrote, "Therefore do not let sin reign in your mortal body, that you should obey it in its lusts" (Romans 6:12).

What could you have done differently if you didn't allow those feeling to consume you?

_____

_____

_____

We win because

we are in Jesus.

Day 4

REMEMBER

> "God doesn't call us to take the wide road, which would be way easier. He asks us to walk the narrow one—the one that includes loss, difficulty, pain, relational conflict, and uncertainty. But we're not alone. I'm so thankful Jesus not only did the hard things Himself, but He also did the hardest thing. He died for us and conquered death so we could live an abundant, full life. With Him, all we do is win." (*The Fight to Flourish*, page 74)

PREPARE

If you are reading along in *The Fight to Flourish* book, read chapters 7, 8, and 9 this week. Capture any statements or phrases that motivated or challenged you and that you'd like to share with the group next week.

_____

_____

_____

_____

JENNIE'S PRAYER FOR YOU

Father, thank You that in the midst of a world of loss and trouble and pain, our relationship with You is the one thing that cannot be taken away. I pray for the beautiful one reading this. Reveal to her Your love in a special way. I pray you cultivate in her a dependence on Your Word as she leans into all that You have for her. And when the enemy throws the fiery darts at her mind and heart, I pray she rejects those thoughts and chooses to believe and stand on Your promises instead. Remind her that You have written her name on the palm of Your hand. And that by Your strength, she can stick to the plan You have laid out for her life. In Jesus' name I pray, amen.

READY, SET, *Live!*

Overview ::

We flourish when we immerse ourselves in the present moment, in the blend of the good and bad.

Review ::

(5-10 minutes)

Share one thing that stood out to you most from last session's video or discussion.

Session Start-up ::

(5 minutes)

LEADER: Read aloud to group.

At times it seems life offers more questions than answers. Why isn't this world a better place? Why do terrible people who do terrible things exist? Why must we have to do life with wretched diseases like cancer or economic recessions or plane crashes or freak accidents? These questions have been debated and argued throughout time. For believers, when we focus more on the "why" than on the "who," we are bound to become cynical, depressed, or hopeless. There's nothing wrong with asking questions. But sometimes the questions are unanswerable this side of heaven. So it becomes more important to fix our attention on the "who." To choose God. And to keep choosing Him.

Second Chronicles 16:9 tells us,

> "The eyes of the LORD search the whole earth in order to strengthen those whose hearts are fully committed to him" (NLT).

God is on the lookout to find people who are following His ways. He wants us to draw near. He wants us to look for and to Him when no answer or reason or logic can satisfy our questions. When we our grounded in this way, we can sustain our focus and our footing even when blindsided by challenges, unexpected news, and sudden disappointment.

Jesus gave great advice about staying focused on the present. He said,

> "Therefore do not worry about tomorrow, for tomorrow will worry about its own things" (Matthew 6:34).

When we fret about what tomorrow may bring or are unable to let go of what haunts us from the past, we can't be here, right now. Sometimes the future or the past seems more exciting than where we are in the present. But it's our job to dwell in the place of now. It's where we live. We're over yesterday and tomorrow hasn't arrived yet. We're here, now. Today.

When we engage in everyday life, no matter what it brings, we can be fully engaged in what God has for us. If we're too busy worrying about tomorrow or wishing we could redo yesterday, we might miss the opportunities God has for us in this day. We certainly won't be able to live ready, open to hear from Him, available to speak life over someone, willing to stop in the middle of busy and do something we feel God prompting us to do.

It may be more than distractions that keep us from engaging in the present; it may be our insecurities. Maybe you feel underqualified or overwhelmed and use those feelings to justify passing on an assignment God may have given you. Great news, friend. You're always going to be insufficient by your own standard. We all are. But with Jesus, we can do all things. Even the ones that seem impossible.

Talk About It ::

(5-10 minutes)
How easy/hard is it to trust God's sovereignty in situations that bring pain, heartache, or disappointment?

Session 3 Video ::

(14 minutes)
Watch the session 3 video. While viewing the video, use the outline and spaces below to record key ideas or any thoughts you want to remember.

VIDEO TEACHING NOTES

- The good and the hard walk hand in hand.

- Psalm 30:11–12 NLT

   "You have turned my mourning into joyful dancing.
   You have taken away my clothes of mourning and clothed me with joy,
   that I might sing praises to you and not be silent.
   O LORD my God, I will give you thanks forever!"

- 2 Chronicles 16:9 NLT

   "The eyes of the LORD search the whole earth in order to strengthen those whose hearts are fully committed to him."

- The key to living this flourishing life is keeping our eyes fixed on the one who designed us, created us, and has such a beautiful purpose and plan for our lives.

- There is a power in being in the present, being right here right now, no matter what is happening around you.

- God has something special and beautiful for you right now in the beauty of the blend of hard and good.

- We can live ready as God gives us opportunities to show others His love.

- We have what it takes.

- Story of Moses (Exodus 3)

- God is interested in our willingness, not what we have done or could do for Him.

- It's possible to miss Jesus.

Small Group Discussion ::

(30-40 minutes)

LEADER: Read aloud each numbered prompt. Select a volunteer to read the Scripture.

1. In the video teaching, Jennie talks about how the terrible and the beautiful can coexist. She considers how there can be dancing in mourning, joy in heartache, peace in chaos.

   Give an example of how you have experienced this truth in your life.

2. One of God's specialties is turning bad situations into opportunities for grace, mercy, renewal, and healing. Share about a painful or dark time that God had somehow mined for good. What impact did it have on your life? How did it change your perspective?

3. How can you walk alongside someone who is suffering and having a hard time connecting with God?

4. In the video teaching, Jennie says that the key to living a flourishing life is keeping our eyes fixed on the One who designed us, created us, and has a beautiful purpose and plan for our lives. Read aloud 2 Chronicles 16:9:

"The eyes of the LORD search the whole earth in order to strengthen those whose hearts are fully committed to him" (NLT).

Reflect on this Scripture for a moment and then share how this verse encourages or challenges you as you fight to flourish.

5. It's easy to enjoy life when it's stress-, worry-, and care-free. But God wants us to enjoy life every day. Read John 10:10:

"The thief does not come except to steal, and to kill, and to destroy. I have come that they may have life, and that they may have it more abundantly."

God wants us to have an abundant life. One that overflows with joy. How can you begin to enjoy life in all seasons? (Tip: Think about not only seasons of obvious hardship but also seasons that feel boring or empty.)

6. How often do you allow your insecurities to dictate what you do or don't do for God? When did God come through even though you may have felt unworthy or unqualified? What can you do, starting today, to step out of your feelings of inadequacy and into the confidence of Christ?

7. When life gets busy and distractions are many, how do you keep from missing Jesus in the present moment?

Wrap It Up ::

(5 minutes)

LEADER: Read the following paragraph and select a reader to close the group in prayer. She can use her own words or be guided by the ideas below:

Today we have learned that we can find good in the difficulty, beauty in the struggle. Even hard things have the power to help us flourish because the fighting and the flourishing are meant to blend together. We can only experience such beauty when we immerse ourselves in the present, in whatever moment we find ourselves. When we are willing to be used by God, He will arm us with whatever we need to get the job done—and do it well.

Let's close this time together in prayer. Here are some ideas from this session that can guide your conversation with God:

- Thank Him for walking with you in every step of the fight.
- Ask Him to help change your perspective on a situation that feels overwhelming or daunting.
- Surrender any unwillingness you have struggled with in allowing God to use you.
- Thank Him for His great love that is unconditional, unwavering, unending, and has nothing to do with our performance.

Dig Deeper

PERSONAL STUDY / SESSION 3

Day 1

STUDY

I'm sure you've heard some version of the following statement: "Live in the present moment." It's such a vital truth. And it seems we are reminded of this everywhere, from our fitness classes to our devotional apps to social media posts. Okay, we get it. But why is it so hard to do? So often we get bogged down by what happened yesterday, or we worry about what will or won't happen tomorrow. But when we absorb the present moment, even if it's hard, we can live how God intended us to live, right here, right now.

The Greek New Testament has two words for "time." One is *chronos*, which is a quantifiable measure of time, like seconds, minutes, and hours—the time on a clock. The other is *kairos*, which means the right, critical, or opportune moment. You can flesh this out to mean the present moment. Now.

When we live by *chronos* time, we are unattached to what's happening in the moment. We're looking ahead to the next thing or wondering how many things we can cram in the rest of the day. Living by *kairos* opens us up to the opportunity of what God wants to do in and for us now. In a sense, we transcend time. When we absorb where we are right here and right now, we enter the realm of *kairos*. In this space, we can listen for God even in the midst of chaos around us. We can forget about yesterday and stop thinking about tomorrow. We can be open to enjoying and embracing whatever or whoever is set before us.

REFLECT

Journal your thoughts about how you have lived up until today, either through the task-master of *chronos* or through the life-changing filter of *kairos*?

List some obstacles that keep you from being in the moment.

Think about a moment that you fully engaged in the present. Write about it. What happened? Who were you with? What were you doing? How did it feel? What did you learn from the experience?

Take a few moments to check in with yourself right now. Identify the moment you are in. Describe your surroundings. Who is around? How are you feeling? What thoughts are swimming in your head?

What habits can you practice starting today to become more aware of the present moment? This could include things such as powering off your smartphone before bed, spending less time on social media, calling people instead of texting them, etc. For the next thirty days, challenge yourself to commit to these habits.

When we absorb the present moment, even if it's hard, we can live how God intended us to live, right here, right now.

Day 2

REVIEW

Review chapters 7, 8, and 9 in *The Fight to Flourish*.

REMEMBER

"Have you ever wanted to rush through a time in your life to get to the next level? To avoid this heartache, this inconvenience, this pain, and magically end up somewhere easier, less demanding, and less overwhelming? We want to skip over the hard stuff; it's as though we're doing sit-ups in PE class and stop the moment the coach turns her back, only to act like we were doing them all along when she turns around again. (I'm not necessarily speaking from experience. Okay, fine—I did this last week in a spin class during the part where we work out our arms.)

"When we skip over the work God has for us, we shortchange ourselves. We get to the next season but without the tools, extra points, and spare lives we need to stay there. When you immerse yourself in where you are right now, God will give you the ability to push through. It's in this tension that we grow." (*The Fight to Flourish*, page 109)

REFLECT

Write down what you have learned, a breakthrough you experienced, or a shift in perspective from this video or discussion. Prepare to share with the group next week.

What Scripture spoke to you most this week? Try to memorize it. Write it down below and then put it on an index card or sticky note and place it wherever you spend some alone time each day (the bathroom, your car, on a kitchen window or laptop cover).

When you immerse yourself in where you are right now, God will give you the ability to push through. It's in this tension that we grow.

Day 3

STUDY

Read Exodus 3, the story of God calling Moses.

List the five excuses Moses gave God for not immediately accepting the call:

◆ Excuse #1: _____

◆ Excuse #2: _____

◆ Excuse #3: _____

◆ Excuse #4: _____

◆ Excuse #5: _____

REFLECT

What excuses above do you relate to or find yourself telling God?

_____

_____

_____

In *The Fight to Flourish*, pages 123–124, Jennie writes:

"How often do we find ourselves wanting to run in the opposite direction or hide in bed, under the covers? The idea that unwillingness is actually disobedience is a game changer for me. Whether or not I feel worthy or qualified or able, I want to say yes to God. I want to be in such a place of trusting Him that I am willing to do what He has asked me to do, whether it makes sense to me or not.

"I pray that we would always have willing hearts. If God's got a job for us, He is going to give us the strength to do it, even and especially if we feel we can't get it done."

Write about a situation in which you felt unqualified or undeserving but through your obedience to God, you got the job done.

_____

_____

_____

You're always going to be insufficient by your own standard. We all are. But with Jesus, we can do all things. Even the ones that seem impossible.

Day 4

REMEMBER

"Religion says, 'Do this and then be.' A relationship with Jesus says, 'Be in Christ and then do.' God's love isn't based on you; it's placed on you. You can rest in His love for you and then live, work, lead, and love from that place. Don't strive in your own strength; surrender to the Spirit and His strength." (*The Fight to Flourish*, page 131)

PREPARE

If you are reading along in *The Fight to Flourish*, read chapters 10, 11, and 12 this week. Capture any statements or phrases that motivated or challenged you and that you'd like to share with the group next week.

JENNIE'S PRAYER FOR YOU

Lord God, continue to whisper in this sweet heart's ears all the things You want her to hear. Remind her that You are not looking for perfection, but rather pursuit. May she seek You with all her heart. I pray that You would make her ready for each opportunity to encourage, speak life over, and serve others. Remind her that You have uniquely designed her to love the people in her life right here, right now. I know it's easy, especially if we're in a difficult season, to want to fast forward into the next stage. I pray You would help her see that the waiting is just as important as the destination because that is how we grow in trusting You. Teach her how to immerse her whole heart in whatever she is doing to pour the most into and get the most out of the present moment. If she is surrounded by insecurities, may she come to believe that she has what it takes because she is Yours. In Jesus' name, I pray, amen.

SESSION 4

THE ART
OF LIVING
Beautifully

Overview ::

As we lean into God in this fight to flourish, we discover our inherent need to build and nurture relationships. A life lived in community will spark great things.

Review ::

(5-10 minutes)

Share one thing that stood out to you most from last session's video or discussion.

Session Start-up ::

(5 minutes)

LEADER: Read aloud to group.

Our hearts yearn for connection, for intimacy, to know others and to be known by them. We were created for relationship, first with God and then with others. When Jesus was asked what the greatest commandment was, He answered,

> "'You shall love the Lord your God with all your heart, with all your soul, and with all your mind.' This is the first and great command-ment. And the second is like it: 'You shall love your neighbor as yourself.' On these two commandments hang all the Law and the Prophets" (Matthew 22:37–40).

The directive Jesus gave echoes the sentiment behind Ecclesiastes 4:12,

> "Though one may be overpowered by another, two can withstand him. And a threefold cord is not quickly broken."

Relationships are beautiful. It's also no big secret that they can be difficult. Walking alongside someone—championing, encouraging, challenging, and inspiring them as we go—is not always easy. The struggles of life have a way of overshadowing our character, the woman God created us to be, and in vulnerable moments, we may lash out against or isolate ourselves from the very people we love the most. Only with the power of Jesus pouring through us can we sustain a posture of sweetness and humility, especially when we feel anything but that.

Living beautifully means connecting with others in positive and meaningful ways. To live with one another not just on the surface, but to be rooted in depth, offering transparency when appropriate and being genuine in our spirits. We can be a light in the darkness to those who need it. We can be a welcome mat to those who don't know Jesus. We can be a coach to someone who needs to be cheered on to finish her race.

Having a humble, gentle, and sweet spirit doesn't just apply to the ones closest to us. If we are to be salt to the earth, we must see people in and around our communities. Be kind. Practice self-control. Smile instead of complaining while standing in a long check-out line. Be respectful. Ask someone who is struggling how you can help. Give someone a hug. Pay a compliment. You never know how such a simple gesture can make a lasting impact.

When we're going through a trying season, it can be tempting to shut down and isolate. But when we let others into our lives and share with them our hearts, we birth power, strength, and beauty. When women unite and love and serve God together, like you do, they become unstoppable.

Talk About It ::

(5-10 minutes)
In what way(s) does our faith stretch, grow, or get recharged when we are in relationship with others?

Session 4 Video ::

(13 minutes)
Watch the session 4 video. While viewing the video, use the outline and spaces below to record key ideas or any thoughts you want to remember.

VIDEO TEACHING NOTES

◆ We are stronger together.

◆ God wants to heal us and let Him use our pain for His glory.

◆ Psalm 16:6

"The lines have fallen to me in pleasant places;
Yes, I have a good inheritance."

◆ I want a natural resting face of sweetness and kindness.

◆ 1 Peter 3:4 (THE MESSAGE)

"Cultivate inner beauty, the gentle, gracious kind that God delights in."

- Kind eyes start in the soul.

- Hebrews 10:24–25

    "And let us consider one another in order to stir up love and good works, not forsaking the assembling of ourselves together, as is the manner of some, but exhorting one another, and so much the more as you see the Day approaching."

- God has called us to stir up the sweetness in our souls.

- We are meant to do life together.

- 1 Peter 4:8

    "For love will cover a multitude of sins."

◆ 1 Peter 5:5 NIV

"Clothe yourselves with humility toward one another, because, 'God opposes the proud but shows favor to the humble.'"

◆ Proverbs 11:14

"In the multitude of counselors there is safety."

◆ You find strength when you gather with others in a local church.

◆ Romans 12:9–11 TPT

"Let the inner movement of your heart always be to love one another, and never play the role of an actor wearing a mask. Despise evil and embrace everything that is good and virtuous. Be devoted to tenderly loving your fellow believers as members of one family. Try to outdo yourselves in respect and honor of one another. Be enthusiastic to serve the Lord, keeping your passion toward him boiling hot! Radiate with the glow of the Holy Spirit and let him fill you with excitement as you serve him."

Small Group Discussion ::

(30-40 minutes)

LEADER: Read aloud each numbered prompt. Select a volunteer to read the Scripture and content from *The Fight to Flourish* book.

1. In the book *The Fight to Flourish*, page 146, Jennie writes:

    "My heart is to be at my best with my husband, my kids, and those closest to me, but at times I'm at my worst with them. The moment I speak with a snippy tone or have an ungrateful look, I know it. I feel it. I hate it. And I immediately regret it. Moments like these make me evaluate how I respond to people and why.

    "I can't control others or their responses, but I can control myself. I love how Lance Witt, author of *High Impact Teams*, puts it: 'When it comes to your life, you hold the position of CLO: chief life officer. That doesn't mean you control everything in your world, but it does mean you are responsible for leading yourself.' I am the CLO of my life—no one else's. As hard as it may feel in the moment, I can control my attitude, my facial expressions, the atmosphere of my heart.

    "I don't have to let my frustration turn into frostiness. Instead of immediately reacting to someone negatively, with critique or judgment, I want to be a woman who responds strongly with compassion, understanding, and sweetness."

    How does attitude impact relationships in general? How about for you personally?

2. In the video teaching, Jennie dives into the importance of stirring up sweetness in our lives. Read Colossians 3:12–13:

> "Therefore, as the elect of God, holy and beloved, put on tender mercies, kindness, humility, meekness, longsuffering; bearing with one another, and forgiving one another, if anyone has a complaint against another; even as Christ forgave you, so you also must do."

Share a time when you tried to fight against an urge to respond harshly to someone. Did you choose to reflect the heart behind the above Scripture? What was the outcome? How can this experience prepare you for a future one?

3. Proverbs 18:21 tells us,

> "Death and life are in the power of the tongue."

How intentional are you in using your words to edify others? How about on social media? How do you hold yourself accountable to ensuring your posts or comments bring life? How does it make you feel when Christians post negatively?

4. Why is pride so harmful in relationships? How does humility work against the destructive force of pride?

Read 1 Peter 5:5 NIV,

"Clothe yourselves with humility toward one another, because, 'God opposes the proud but shows favor to the humble.'"

List aloud practical ways you can "clothe yourselves with humility."

5. A survey by the Barna Group* showed that the number one reason spiritual seekers attend a church is community. The top three reasons include:

 • Knowing that everyone will be welcoming
 • Making friends and nurturing friendships
 • Support during difficult times

What does this tell you about the importance of developing a community of believers? Do you feel this need is satisfied in your church?

6. Read Ephesians 4:12–16:

" . . . for the equipping of the saints for the work of ministry, for the edifying of the body of Christ, till we all come to the unity of the faith and of the knowledge of the Son of God, to a perfect man, to the measure of the stature of the fullness of Christ; that we should no longer be children, tossed to and fro and carried about with every

---

* http://s3.amazonaws.com/Website_Properties/news-media/press-center/documents/seeker_study_2017_info-graphic.pdf

wind of doctrine, by the trickery of men, in the cunning craftiness of deceitful plotting, but, speaking the truth in love, may grow up in all things into Him who is the head—Christ—from whom the whole body, joined and knit together by what every joint supplies, according to the effective working by which every part does its share, causes growth of the body for the edifying of itself in love."

Why is it important that the local and global church be united? In what ways do you see division in the church? In what ways do you see solidarity?

7. Jennie teaches about the value of vulnerability in nurturing relationships. How easy or hard is it to be vulnerable and transparent in your relationships? Why? Is there a time/place/reason why we shouldn't be vulnerable with others?

Wrap It Up ::

(5 minutes)

LEADER: Read the following paragraph and select a reader to close the group in prayer. She can use her own words or be guided by the ideas below:

In this session we learned the art of living beautifully with other women walking alongside us. We were created to be in relationship with others. This means we need to cultivate vulnerability, transparency, and deep friendships. We also must choose to engage with others with a sweet attitude, being quick to forgive, show mercy, and display kindness.

Let's close in prayer. Here are some ideas from this session that can guide your conversation with God:

- Thank God for surrounding you with a community of women like those in your small group to help you become the woman you are created to be.
- Ask God to help you nurture the right relationships and be open to forming new ones.
- Ask for forgiveness for being catty, judgmental, or gossipy toward another woman.
- Thank God for the wisdom and insight He's given you through the outlet of a friendship.

Dig Deeper

PERSONAL STUDY / SESSION 4

Day 1

STUDY

Read Lamentations 3:22–25:

> "Through the Lord's mercies we are not consumed, because His compassions fail not. They are new every morning; great is Your faithfulness. 'The Lord is my portion,' says my soul, 'Therefore I hope in Him!' The Lord is good to those who wait for Him, to the soul who seeks Him."

What word or phrase strikes you in this passage? Why?

_____

_____

_____

_____

List four attributes of God found in this Scripture.

1 _____

2. _____

3. _____

4. _____

Review the attributes you just wrote down. Now think about your everyday life. In what way(s) do you exhibit these traits with others, from those closest to you to strangers you encounter on the subway, in the gym, or at the coffeeshop?

_____

_____

_____

How do you cultivate kindness in your world? How do you respond to people who are unkind? Are you kind to the people closest to you—friends and family who know you really well? What is uniquely challenging about being their cheerleader?

_____

_____

_____

_____

Read Hebrews 10:24:

> "And let us consider one another in order to stir up love and good works."

The Greek word used for stir is *paroxusmos*, which means to provoke or incite (to goodness). We ought to do more than just love and do good works, we must also help to stir up others to do the same. Wow! That's powerful! And challenging.

REFLECT

Write down two ways you do this in your everyday life. If you're struggling to answer this question, list two ways that you could start inspiring kindness in others.

1. _____
2. _____

In *The Fight to Flourish*, page 147, Jennie writes:

"If God's kindness leads us to repentance (Romans 2:4), it means He looks at us with kind eyes. He doesn't respond to the ugly things we do or say with a frown, or with disappointment, or with blame. He looks at us with love in His eyes. If God can look at me this way, while I'm still in the midst of all my sin and flaws and failures, how can I not look at my husband, my children, and the people I encounter in the same way?

"I'd say most of us women love making our eyes pretty. We apply shimmery eye shadow, mascara, eyeliner, and eyelash extensions to try to make our eyes sparkle. We also dab on eye creams to try to lessen the blow of the aging process. Now, I'm not an anti-makeup-kind of girl and I think it's important to take care of the skin we're in, but no amount of glittery makeup or faux eyelashes can make our eyes kind. This happens on the inside. It's a heart issue. Kind eyes get their running start from the soul."

Our goal in life is to become more and more like Jesus. Some days may seem like a win while other days are ripe with failure and mistakes. Thank God for grace! One of the most life-giving ways we can begin to reflect the image of Christ is to treat people with kindness, sow generously, and stir sweetness into our attitudes. And the best starting point to live this out is to remember who God is and what He has done for us.

When's the last time you thanked God for who He is and what He has done for you? Write down a prayer expressing your gratitude.

_____

_____

_____

_____

_____

_____

As hard as it may feel in the moment, I can control my attitude, my facial expressions, the atmosphere of my heart.

Day 2

REVIEW

Review chapters 10, 11, and 12 in *The Fight to Flourish*.

REMEMBER

"The Enemy wants us to hide our hearts from others. He whispers in our ears anything he can use to keep us isolated and disconnected. You're the only one struggling with this; other people won't understand and will judge you. Or maybe, If you tell her what you're really feeling, she'll never want to be your friend. God knows the power and healing that happens when we speak up, and so should we. When we bring others into our pain, we position ourselves to receive wisdom, insight, and a different perspective that we wouldn't have gained otherwise. (*The Fight to Flourish*, pages 141and 143)

REFLECT

Write down what you have learned, a breakthrough you experienced, or a shift in perspective from this video session or discussion. Prepare to share with the group next week.

What Scripture spoke to you most this week? Try to memorize it. Write it down below and then put it on an index card or sticky note and place it wherever you spend some alone time each day (the bathroom, your car, on a kitchen window or laptop cover).

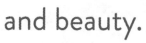

When we let others into

our lives and share with

them our hearts, we

birth power, strength,

and beauty.

Day 3

STUDY

According to a Barna study, 62 percent of adults have anywhere from two to five close friends. Yet one in five people is lonely. While some of us are content with a couple of friends and others love to be surrounded by a tribe, the fact is having friends is a positive thing. Science confirms this. People who have a strong network of friends suffer less stress and live longer. Julianne Holt-Lunstad, professor of psychology and head of a study at Brigham Young University, even wrote that "Not having a social support network can be a higher death risk than obesity or leading a sedentary life without exercise."* Who knew having a girl squad was actually good for your health?

Friends are important. They love, support, encourage, strengthen, and challenge us. We learn and grow from them. They bring joy, laughter and smiles into our lives. No doubt, we are wired for relationships. But have you noticed how difficult it can be to find or maintain friendships, especially as we become older? This just means we must be intentional in cultivating our relationships.

REFLECT

What purpose do friends serve in your life?

_____

_____

_____

---

* https://www.huffingtonpost.co.uk/2014/09/04/10-facts-about-friendship_n_5764448.html?guccounter=1&guce_referrer=aHR0cHM6Ly93d3cuZ29vZ2xlLmNvbS8&guce_referrer_sig=AQAAAG-Q3jy1yTHCD0K-DKCD-jBtanJ5861HgmbC8ksTRll707m9o9kHIWlnSpfDFQedaJ9tx7nmV3dHoPnO_RaLd0w7qUl4W-k-dNGXPKetQc6tukVuBPSbYC_4LSLWNpB-IFPD3huSWwH73Ycv4ovcG3L8FHgFOchhE1fAuLKXVxlu

On a scale of one to ten, 10 being the highest and 1 being the lowest, how much of a priority do you place on friendships? Mark it on the scale below.

1	2	3	4	5	6	7	8	9	10

Let's rate your score!

If you scored 1–3 on the scale, it's time to consider growing deeper with others and cultivating meaningful relationships. Begin to journal the reason why you place such a low value on friendships (i.e., lack of time, trust issues).

Read Ecclesiastes 4:9–10:

> "Two are better than one, because they have a good reward for their labor. For if they fall, one will lift up his companion. But woe to him who is alone when he falls, for he has no one to help him up."

What comes to mind when you read this verse? When is the last time you took a hard hit in your life and someone helped you get back on track? How did this make you feel?

Challenge: If you've been burned by a friend and, as a result, have distanced yourselves from others or are having difficulty being vulnerable for any other reason, I invite you to bring this pain to God. Ask Him to heal your hurt and help you recognize that He created you for relationships. Then, for the next thirty days, pray that God softens your heart and opens doors that allow you to meet someone who could be a friend or to strengthen a friendship that's on your heart.

If you just moved to a new city and have found it hard to make new friends, write down a prayer for God to help you meet the right people. Then, give yourself the opportunity to meet others. Join a small group at church or a fitness or volunteer organization in your community. Take initiative and reach out to one or two people. See what friendships blossom.

Spoiler alert: You're probably not going to jump into a BFF relationship with someone you just met. Friendships evolve over time. Relieve yourself of the pressure to find a tribe in a week and allow relationships to unfold organically.

If you scored 4–6 on the scale, you definitely value friendships, but for whatever reason you're not totally sold. Maybe you just don't have time. Maybe running your own business, juggling a full course load, chasing little ones all day, or chauffeuring older kids to practices leaves you with zero margin to hang out with a friend for coffee or chat on the phone for twenty minutes. Or maybe you've found friendships to be complicated. Maybe you're discouraged because you tend to give more than you get, or you feel like you're always the one reaching out or connecting. Friends, like humans, aren't perfect. There are ebbs and flows in relationships. Some friendships are deeper than others. And sometimes one person feels more connected than the other.

Read 1 John 1:3–4:

> " . . . that which we have seen and heard we declare to you, that you also may have fellowship with us; and truly our fellowship is with the Father and with His Son Jesus Christ. And these things we write to you that your joy may be full."

The author is saying that fellowship with others plus fellowship with God equals a life full of joy.

How does this Scripture remind you of the benefits of investing in a network of support? What have you experienced when you coupled a growing relationship with Jesus with a circle of faith-filled friends?

_____

_____

_____

Challenge: If you have a packed calendar and little to zero margin, take another look. See where you can squeeze in an hour to connect with a friend you haven't seen or talked to in a while. Go for a walk together. Grab dinner or a coffee. Make time to nurture friendship.

If friendships seem too complicated to navigate, focus on one or two people in your life who you can commit to nurturing a close connection. If you're feeling like you are doing all the giving, maybe it's time to have a heart-to-heart. Importantly, pray that God opens your eyes to the friendships you need to hold in higher esteem. Ask Him to help you be a better friend. Write down this prayer.

_____

_____

_____

_____

If you scored 7–10 on the scale, well done! You probably have a solid support network that you appreciate and need. You understand the significance of Proverbs 18:24: "A man who has friends must himself be friendly, but there is a friend who sticks closer than a brother." You are likely a loyal friend and blessed to have a loyal squad or tribe.

Challenge: Think of a friend who can be described as loving and loyal, truth-telling and grace-filled, supportive and challenging. Write her name down. Do something nice for her today. Send her a sweet text, drop a note in the mail, or invite her out for brunch and tell her how much you appreciate her!

_____

_____

_____

Living beautifully

means connecting with

others in positive and

meaningful ways.

Day 4

REMEMBER

"When we connect with one another with vulnerability, when we gather with the intent to lift each other up, to speak life, and to cheer each other on, something special happens. We empower one another to keep running, to keep growing, to keep blooming. We help unveil the truth that it's possible to flourish beautifully right where God has us." (*The Fight to Flourish*, page 168)

PREPARE

If you are reading along in *The Fight to Flourish*, read chapters 13, 14, and 15 this week. Capture any statements or phrases that motivated or challenged you and that you'd like to share with the group next week.

JENNIE'S PRAYER FOR YOU

Father in heaven, thank You for the new mercies You pour over us morning after morning. I pray for the one reading these words today, that she would reflect to others the kindness and warmth You have shown her. Thank you that the weight is not on her to be sweet and courageous and of service, but it's about You empowering her to flourish in her spirit and in her relationships. I pray that in the same way she is intentional about choosing her fresh outfit for the day, You help her put on love, even and especially toward the ones hardest to love. May she have a girl squad to call her own who can encourage, strengthen, and uplift her—and may she do the same for them. Bring the right people into her life who can help build her faith and who she can lean on in times of great difficulty. Allow her to lock arms with women who can help her grow in this life. Give her what she needs to fight for her relationships and to be the friend that you have called her to be. In Jesus' name, I pray, amen.

SHAKE UP YOUR
Life

Overview ::

Having a fresh soul requires a shake-up. Sometimes God does this for us. Sometimes we need to shake up our own lives. When we keep it fresh, we give ourselves the opportunity to embrace front-row living.

Review ::

(5-10 minutes)

Share one thing that stood out to you most from last session's video or discussion.

Session Start-up ::

(5 minutes)

LEADER: Read aloud to group.

Detoxes are all the rage. Spend a week or twenty-one-days sipping on fresh lemonade spiced with pepper and sweetened with maple syrup or munch only on raw, organic fruits and vegetables and watch toxins disappear from your body. While the jury is still out on whether or not cleanses are essential to our health, most of us would admit to needing a powerful spiritual detox every now and again. This might look like finding a new lens with which to view life or evicting, for good, unhealthy habits that may not be helpful to our spiritual life.

There's something about being shaken up in life that brings change, whether we like it or not, whether we made it happen or God orchestrated it. Shake-ups look different for everyone. We may feel God is distant in a season and, having never before experienced that silence before, it might send us in a tailspin—until we remember that God loves us unconditionally and deeply and perfectly. Sometimes we watch as life seems to fall apart before our eyes, spurred by loss or disappointment. Maybe a shake-up means God is moving us in a new direction, somewhere we would have never expected or planned.

However we get shaken up in life, there many benefits to getting sucked out of our comfort zones. We grow. We learn. We mature. As we allow God to water us and prune back what we don't need, we become more like Jesus, more of whom we were born to be.

Even if we're moving at a slow pace, or take a few steps back, or get knocked down, we have what it takes to keep our spiritual lives fresh as we continue to fight forward.

When we lean into the resistance that life brings, showing up and then some in the process, pouring into the lives of others, we learn what it means to live in the front row. We can make the most out of our lives, flourishing to capacity, even in and through our pain. Need to make sure you are heading in the right direction? Use your story to point to the revelation and truth of Jesus instead of shine a spotlight on your mistakes in the process.

Talk About It ::

(5-10 minutes)
What does it mean to be shaken up but not taken down?

Session 5 Video ::

(10 minutes)
Watch the session 5 video. While viewing the video, use the outline and spaces below to record key ideas or any thoughts you want to remember.

VIDEO TEACHING NOTES

- We can't vibrantly flourish unless we get shaken.

- We get stronger when we push ourselves harder.

- We can get in a rut when we feel God is giving us the silent treatment.

- When you feel alone in the dark, picture yourself in God's shadow.

- Psalm 91:1–4

  > "He who dwells in the secret place of the Most High
  > Shall abide under the shadow of the Almighty.
  > I will say of the LORD, 'He is my refuge and my fortress;
  > My God, in Him I will trust.'
  > Surely He shall deliver you from the snare of the fowler
  > And from the perilous pestilence.
  > He shall cover you with His feathers,
  > And under His wings you shall take refuge;
  > His truth shall be your shield and buckler."

- Even if God feels far, He is near.

- Keep your relationship with Jesus fresh.

- Story of Caleb (Numbers 13–14)

- Psalm 92:14

    "They [the righteous] still shall bear fruit in old age."

- Trust God and ask Him to do a fresh work in your life.

- Front-row living can take you to a new level as you lean in more.

- Pay attention and see and meet the needs around you.

- Share the unique story God has given you. It's powerful.

- Make the most out of your story.

♦ 1 Peter 1:6

> "In this you greatly rejoice, though now for a little while, if need be, you have been grieved by various trials."

Small Group Discussion ::

(30-40 minutes)

LEADER: Read aloud each numbered prompt. Select a volunteer to read the Scripture and content from *The Fight to Flourish* book.

1. When is the last time you felt shaken up in your life? How did this impact your perspective, growth, or outlook?

2. In the video teaching Jennie says, "If we were just to push ourselves a little bit harder, we could actually become stronger." Name a time where you intentionally took yourself to the next level (physically, mentally, spiritually, or emotionally). How did this make you feel? How did it make you stronger?

3. Do you feel close to God or does He seem distant? What are some spiritual disciplines that can help you feel near to God or strengthen your belief that He is present, even though it may not seem like it?

4. How does faulty religion place the blame on us when we feel God is silent in our lives? Have you experienced this kind of guilt or condemnation?

5. In *The Fight to Flourish*, page 193, Jennie writes:

> "We have the choice to let Jesus shake us up or to stay in our comfort zones. Not looking to Jesus, not letting Him change us with His Word and with the trials we face, keeps us stagnant. We won't grow and we won't mature.
>
> "But the good news is that we can do something about it.
>
> "When you vigorously shake a natural juice, the separation goes away. The good stuff doesn't stay at the bottom, and the bland stuff doesn't stay at the top. The sediment and water blend.
>
> "Allowing God to shake us up is truly fresh living."

Talk about what "fresh life living" can look like in your life.

6. How do you resist or fight against the temptation to allow boredom and stagnation to invade your spiritual walk?

7. Read Ephesians 2:10,

"For we are His workmanship, created in Christ Jesus for good works, which God prepared beforehand that we should walk in them."

Wrap Up ::

(5 minutes)

LEADER: Read the following paragraph and select a reader to close the group in prayer. She can use her own words or be guided by the ideas below:

Today we have learned that being shaken up is a good thing. It can pull us out of a rut, allowing us to enter the realm of fresh life living. As we continue to look up in the middle of tough times when God seems silent or tough times come, we can view our struggles as nutrients to help us continue growing in the right direction. Fresh faith leads to a fresh life.

Let's close our time together in prayer. Here are some ideas from this session that can guide our conversation with God:

- Invite God to shake you up out of a rut or stagnant place and cultivate in you a mindset to work hard, lean in, and put in extra effort.

- Thank God that His love is beyond comprehension, never changes, and is unconditional, no matter how we feel.

- Ask Him to reveal areas in your life that may keep you from being fully united with Him.

- Ask Him to help you be aware of and pay attention to opportunities that meet the needs of others.

Dig Deeper

PERSONAL STUDY / SESSION 5

* * * * ⚡ * * * *

Day 1

STUDY

Most Jesus followers would admit to experiencing seasons when they feel disconnected from God. We may engage in spiritual disciplines such as prayer and going to church, but it can still feel like He is silent. Our prayers seem like monologues that drone on with no response. The warm fuzzies that once enveloped us during sweet times of worship are absent. It may feel as though God has forgotten about or abandoned us. These times can be spiritually frustrating, disappointing even. But He is with us even when we do not feel like He is.

Read James 4:8:

"Draw near to God and He will draw near to you."

This is a promise God gives us that He will not break. This is true despite our feelings. How can this verse encourage you during the times it seems God is silent?

_____

_____

_____

When we learn to trust God, when we don't feel or hear from Him, we strengthen our faith. We increase our spiritual stamina and endurance. We move from a faith based on feelings to a faith based on truth.

Read the story about Lazarus in the Gospel of John:

> "Now Jesus loved Martha and her sister and Lazarus. So, when He heard that he was sick, He stayed two more days in the place where He was. Then after this He said to the disciples, 'Let us go to Judea again.'
>
> "The disciples said to Him, 'Rabbi, lately the Jews sought to stone You, and are You going there again?'
>
> "Jesus answered, 'Are there not twelve hours in the day? If anyone walks in the day, he does not stumble, because he sees the light of this world. But if one walks in the night, he stumbles, because the light is not in him.' These things He said, and after that He said to them, 'Our friend Lazarus sleeps, but I go that I may wake him up.'
>
> "Then His disciples said, 'Lord, if he sleeps he will get well.' However, Jesus spoke of his death, but they thought that He was speaking about taking rest in sleep.
>
> "Then Jesus said to them plainly, 'Lazarus is dead. And I am glad for your sakes that I was not there, that you may believe. Nevertheless let us go to him'" (John 11:5–15).

Jesus and Lazarus were close friends. Jesus loved him. And yet, when Jesus heard his friend was sick, He did something unusual. Although He was only a few villages away, Jesus didn't drop everything to rush and heal Lazarus. Jesus stayed put. And not just for a few minutes to wrap up whatever He was doing or make arrangements to get to Lazarus. He stayed where He was for two more days.

Put yourself in Mary or Martha's shoes. How would it make you feel knowing your brother was sick, and would die, and Jesus never showed up in that moment of crisis? What would you have said to Jesus?

_____

_____

Read the rest of the story:

"Then, when Mary came where Jesus was, and saw Him, she fell down at His feet, saying to Him, 'Lord, if You had been here, my brother would not have died.'

"Therefore, when Jesus saw her weeping, and the Jews who came with her weeping, He groaned in the spirit and was troubled. And He said, 'Where have you laid him?'

"They said to Him, 'Lord, come and see.'

"Jesus wept. Then the Jews said, 'See how He loved him!'

"And some of them said, 'Could not this Man, who opened the eyes of the blind, also have kept this man from dying?' Then Jesus, again groaning in Himself, came to the tomb. It was a cave, and a stone lay against it. Jesus said, 'Take away the stone.'

"And Jesus lifted up His eyes and said, 'Father, I thank You that You have heard Me. And I know that You always hear Me, but because of the people who are standing by I said this, that they may believe that

You sent Me.' Now when He had said these things, He cried with a loud voice, 'Lazarus, come forth!' And he who had died came out bound hand and foot with graveclothes, and his face was wrapped with a cloth. Jesus said to them, 'Loose him, and let him go'" (John 11:32–39, 41–44).

When Jesus finally showed up, He was heartbroken. In His heartbreak, we see the depth of His love. It's the only instance recorded in the Bible of Jesus crying. God may not answer our prayers the way we want, but it's not because He is apathetic about our plight. We may not understand the way He chooses to operate, but He is with us in our brokenness, empathetic with our pain because He loves us.

REFLECT

Have you grown spiritually during a time of silence? Write down your experience. Or, if you have distanced yourself from God during a similar experience, write about that.

How can you live out your faith in another season of silence, knowing that God has not forgotten about you even though life may still hurt?

Read Psalm 62:1,

"Truly my soul silently waits for God; from Him comes my salvation."

If you are feeling discouraged or abandoned right now, how can you allow yourself to trust God instead of drawing back in your faith?

_____

_____

_____

Draw near to God and

He will draw near to

you. (James 4:8)

Day 2

REVIEW

Review chapters 13, 14, and 15 in *The Fight to Flourish*.

REMEMBER

"A seed is planted deep in the soil, far from sunshine and from everything warm and good. Yet the darkness and distance serve a purpose. They create the space needed for growth and maturity. We are very much like seeds in this way. When we feel separated or disconnected from God, we're living in the tension of sanctification, the process between believing in Jesus now and seeing Him later. When we continue to trust Him in the silence, we'll discover that we're actually flourishing in His shadow." (*The Fight to Flourish*, page 187)

REFLECT

Write down what you have learned, a breakthrough you experienced, or a shift in perspective from this video session or discussion. Prepare to share with the group next week.

_____

_____

_____

What Scripture spoke to you most this week? Try to memorize it. Write it down below and then put it on an index card or sticky note and place it wherever you spend some alone time each day (the bathroom, your car, on a kitchen window or laptop cover).

_____

_____

_____

As we allow God to water

us and prune back what we

don't need, we become more

like Jesus, more of whom

we were born to be.

Day 3

STUDY

We each have a story. You may think your story is boring or that nobody wants to hear your story. If this is you, stop right there. If any part of your life includes being changed, shaped, healed, or made whole, it's a story worth telling.

We encourage one another when we share our stories. Paul wrote,

> **"that I may be encouraged together with you by the mutual faith both of you and me" (Romans 1:12).**

And note this doesn't just include the good stuff like the highlight reel we love to post on social media. It includes our failures as well as our triumphs, our losses and our wins, our mistakes and the lessons we learned in the process.

Your story matters, and God wants you to share it with others. We are challenged in 1 Peter 3:15:

> **"Always be ready to give a defense to everyone who asks you a reason for the hope that is in you."**

The word *defense* is another word for *answer*. In other words, be prepared to give an answer for the hope you have in Jesus.

REFLECT

In *The Fight to Flourish*, page 209, Jennie writes:

> "Story is king, as the saying goes. And if we are to help people, part of that means being storytellers. From the time Lenya went home to heaven, we have allowed God to use the pain attached to our story. While it has been an honor to witness countless lives changed, it can sometimes be difficult to be the 'grief experts' helping others walk through their sorrow. To be honest, there have been times when I haven't wanted to put

myself out there and take a phone call or pray with someone in person so I didn't have to revisit my pain. Pretty selfish, right? But I have to fight to be the carrier of the story God has allowed us to have. It's a privilege to be trusted with this pain. So many people walk through similar journeys, but they don't get the honor of sharing it with thousands upon thousands of people. . . . But as much as we may want to crawl in a hole and keep the pain to ourselves, we can't stay there forever. When we trust God, He can do remarkable things in our lives and in the lives of those around us as we share our stories."

When is the last time you told someone your story? What was the outcome?

_____

_____

_____

If you've never done this before, consider writing it down so you have it in your head next time the opportunity presents itself. Below is a framework you can follow and prompts to help craft your story.

- What was your life like before following Jesus? (i.e., What was most important to you? From what person or thing did you find satisfaction? What were some of your biggest struggles?)

_____

_____

_____

_____

- How did you come to enjoy a personal relationship with Jesus?

_____

_____

_____

_____

◆ What was your life like after deciding to trust in Jesus? (What attitudes, mindsets, and beliefs changed? How does a relationship with Him help you cope with or tackle life's challenges or dark moments? How does your faith inform your decisions, actions, behaviors?)

_____

_____

_____

_____

◆ Describe defining moments of your faith. Maybe include a specific time when you have seen God work in your life. Maybe write about how He strengthened you in one of your weakest moments or how His presence got you through a loss or how He is healing you from an addiction.

_____

_____

_____

_____

A few guidelines to follow as you craft your story:

◆ Keep it brief, around three to five minutes.
◆ Steer away from totally religious rhetoric. Don't use Christian buzz words like repentance or born again or washed in the blood unless you explain what you mean. Try not to sound too preachy.
◆ Keep it fresh. God is always adding to your story. Continue to add to this exercise as needed.
◆ Pray for God to give you opportunities in which you can share your story.

Take the first step and share your story this week with a friend or someone you feel needs to experience the hope found in Jesus. Describe how your time together went on the next page.

REFLECT

Fresh faith leads

to a fresh life.

Day 4

REMEMBER

"What is the goal of a flourishing life? That the genuineness of our faith would be proved by the trials that grieve us. That we would point to the revelation of Jesus. That we would live now, fueling our fight through the struggle. What God does in you isn't just for you. As you lean into front-row living, He wants to not just do the beautifying work in you but to work through you to strengthen those around you. Keep showing up; keep standing out. God is up to something." (*The Fight to Flourish*, page 214)

PREPARE

If you are reading along in *The Fight to Flourish*, read chapters 16 and 17 this week. Capture any statements or phrases that motivated or challenged you and that you'd like to share with the group next week.

_____

_____

_____

_____

JENNIE'S PRAYER FOR YOU

Lord God, would You fill this sweet heart afresh with Your Holy Spirit? If she is feeling far from Your presence, I pray You would draw near. Remind her how near You are. You have not left her and You never will. I pray that she looks up and sees how good and faithful You are. Reveal to her what might be dividing her attention away from You and unite her heart to fear Your name. I pray this beautiful woman lives a fresh life, that she is fruitful in all stages. If she is tired or weak or life feels impossible, remind her that You are working in her and You will be faithful to complete what You started. Shake up her heart in a way that won't allow her to be shaken by the trials in this life. Use her pain to transform the lives of others. Create in her a heart that is open to be used in the most difficult of moments to bring help and healing to others. In Jesus' name, I pray, amen.

YOU DON'T FIGHT
Alone

Overview ::

Our journey to become like Jesus may be hard and long, but be encouraged: God has promised us that He will fight for us and finish what He started.

Review ::

(5-10 minutes)

Share one thing that stood out to you most from last session's video or discussion.

Session Start-up ::

(5 minutes)

LEADER: Read aloud to group.

Do you get excited about waiting? Of course not. Waiting at the doctor's office, waiting for our exam results, waiting for the vacation we spent so much time and energy to plan can be frustrating. This is especially true as we are waiting for God to show up in a challenging situation. Wherever God has called you to, there will be waiting of some kind. Even if you were to follow the seemingly better option, there would be waiting there too. It's part of the process of flourishing.

Psalm 32:24 (TPT) offers great advice:

> "So cheer up! Take courage all you who love him. Wait for him to break through for you, all who trust in him!"

This Scripture gives us a promise. God will "break through" for those who trust Him. None of us know exactly what that looks like or when it will happen or even if it will happen this side of heaven, but that's the point of trusting.

So when we're tired, when we feel like we've been waiting forever, what do we do? We run! God calls us to run with endurance—to withstand pain, trusting Jesus to the very end, even if our sides are cramped up and our legs are on fire. We keep our eyes on Jesus as we run because He has gone before us and has already won the race. A better life is waiting for us, an eternal one, our forever home. With God, there is always more in this life and the next.

We're not running and fighting without a purpose. Nor are we doing these things alone. God loves you. He cares for you. He is with you. And He will fight for you. He encourages you with the same words He told Moses centuries ago,

> "The LORD will fight for you, and you shall hold your peace" (Exodus 14:14).

Your part? Believe Him. Trust Him. Keep your hands up in surrender and keep moving forward.

Talk About It ::

(5-10 minutes)

How does the idea of having eternal life through Jesus inform your actions, beliefs, and decisions on earth?

Session 6 Video ::

(11 minutes)

Watch the session 6 video. While viewing the video, use the outline and spaces below to record key ideas or any thoughts you want to remember.

VIDEO TEACHING NOTES

♦ Jesus came to this earth so that we could have an abundant, flourishing life.

- Galatians 6:9–10

  "And let us not grow weary while doing good, for in due season we shall reap if we do not lose heart. Therefore, as we have opportunity, let us do good to all, especially to those who are of the household of faith."

- Each of us has a longing for our home in heaven.

- Hebrews 12:1–2

  "Therefore we also, since we are surrounded by so great a cloud of witnesses, let us lay aside every weight, and the sin which so easily ensnares us, and let us run with endurance the race that is set before us, looking unto Jesus, the author and finisher of our faith, who for the joy that was set before Him endured the cross, despising the shame, and has sat down at the right hand of the throne of God."

- We are meant to run with endurance.

+ Exodus 14:13–14

> "And Moses said to the people, "Do not be afraid. Stand still, and see the salvation of the LORD, which He will accomplish for you today. For the Egyptians whom you see today, you shall see again no more forever. The LORD will fight for you, and you shall hold your peace."

+ We are not fighting forward alone. God is in our corner.

+ 2 Corinthians 4:16

> "Therefore we do not lose heart. Even though our outward man is perishing, yet the inward man is being renewed day by day."

+ We are meant to flourish through the strength and power of the Holy Spirit.

+ We are created to be an active participant in our lives.

◆ The temptation to want to disengage or opt out can be really strong, but those are the moments that though you can't see it, God is at work.

Small Group Discussion ::

(30-40 minutes)

LEADER: Read aloud each numbered prompt. Select a volunteer to read the content from *The Fight to Flourish*.

1. In the video teaching Jennie encourages us with this: "The temptation to want to disengage or opt out can be really strong, but those are the moments that though you can't see it, God is at work."

   Share about a time that you wanted to quit something that you felt God had called you to do. How did you handle the temptation to give up? What was the outcome?

2. In *The Fight to Flourish*, page 220, Jennie writes:

   > "Wherever God has called you to, there will be waiting of some kind. Even if you were to follow the seemingly better option, there would be waiting there too. Starting fresh somewhere else or with someone else won't be as easy as you think.
   >
   > "So stay where you are and don't rush the process. Don't try to get the SparkNotes edition of your life or the FastPass through the difficulty. There's no pushing past the growth of a seed. You just have to wait."

Talk about an experience in which you had to wait much longer for something than you expected. What did you learn about the waiting process? How can you encourage someone who feels stuck in that place?

3. When we believe and trust in Jesus, we receive the hope of heaven. Talk about a time when you or someone you know experienced a loss without the hope of Jesus. What was this experience like?

4. How has your view of heaven changed as a result of reading this book? What are you most looking forward to when you get there?

5. In the video teaching, through telling the story of Moses, Jennie reminds us that God fights for us. We are not alone in this race. He is in our corner and, more than that, He is packing punches on our behalf. In her book, pages 234–235, she also writes:

> "When we choose to follow Jesus, we inherit the power of God. In a boxing match, a fighter's coach is able to be in the ring with his boxer only when the boxer is not fighting. But in life, God is always with us, giving us Captain Marvel style power punches. Not only does he empower us to keep showing up and building our endurance but He is also strong in our weakness."

Talk about a time you fought for a particular outcome you believed God wanted for your life or for someone else. How did you experience His Captain Marvel style power punches during that time?

6. How has this teaching changed your perspective on what a flourishing life looks like? Discuss how you defined a flourishing life at the beginning of this study and what it means for you now.

Wrap It Up ::

(5 minutes)

LEADER: Read the following paragraph and select a volunteer to close the group in prayer. She can use her own words or be guided by the ideas below:

In this session, we have learned that as we fight forward and wait for God to transform us into the women He has created us to be through His power, we can live in expectation. Life on this earth may not grant us every desire we long for or the answer to every prayer we whisper, but we serve a God of eternity. He has prepared for us a home in heaven, where one day everything will be made right and perfect.

Let's close in prayer. Here are some ideas from this session that can guide your conversation with God:

- Thank Him for His presence and fighting power in every situation.
- Ask Him to fill you with hope that is absent in light of your present situation.
- Ask Him to give you strength and courage to keep serving, giving, living, and loving.
- Thank God for the gift of heaven, which promises an eternal life beyond the messy world we live in.

Dig Deeper

PERSONAL STUDY / SESSION 6

◆ - - ◆ - - ◆ - - ◆ ⚡ ◆ - - ◆ - - ◆ - - ◆

Day 1

STUDY

Read Psalm 130 out loud:

> Out of the depths I have cried to You, O LORD;
> LORD, hear my voice!
> Let Your ears be attentive
> To the voice of my supplications.
>
> If You, LORD, should mark iniquities,
> O LORD, who could stand?
> But there is forgiveness with You,
> That You may be feared.
>
> I wait for the LORD, my soul waits,
> And in His word I do hope.
> My soul waits for the LORD
> More than those who watch for the morning—
> Yes, more than those who watch for the morning.

> O Israel, hope in the LORD;
> For with the LORD there is mercy,
> And with Him is abundant redemption.
> And He shall redeem Israel
> From all his iniquities.

This psalm begins with a desperate cry. Write down your prayer to God in whatever situation you are facing.

_____

_____

_____

_____

After the author of this psalm cries out, he waits and hopes. Write down what the waiting process has looked like for you. Take your time with this. Express your raw emotions. Don't worry, God can handle your honesty.

_____

_____

_____

_____

Now, write down what it looks like to hope in the Lord who overwhelms you with mercy and abundant redemption. List any Scripture that has encouraged you in this process. Here's a few you can start with:

Psalm 86:15: "But You, O LORD, are a God full of compassion, and gracious, longsuffering and abundant in mercy and truth."

Psalm 103:1–5: "Bless the LORD, O my soul; and all that is within me, bless His holy name! Bless the LORD, O my soul, and forget not all His benefits: Who forgives all your iniquities, who heals all your diseases, who redeems your life from destruction, who crowns you with lovingkindness and tender mercies, who satisfies your mouth with good things, so that your youth is renewed like the eagle's."

Isaiah 40:31: "But those who wait on the LORD shall renew their strength; they shall mount up with wings like eagles, they shall run and not be weary, they shall walk and not faint."

REFLECT

I'm sure you've heard the statement, "God is never late, but He is always on time." Even though this adage may not placate our impatience or fulfill our longing, there is truth in it. Most of us want what we want when we want it. When we struggle with addiction or illness or any other life circumstance that forces us to pray desperate prayers, the frustration of waiting is legit. And the questions never stop coming.

- When am I going to get the promotion?
- When is my marriage going to be better?
- Why can't I just quit smoking?
- Why doesn't God just heal my autistic son?

We wait. And wait. And wait. And nothing seems to be happening. The promotion goes to another employee. Our marriage is still stale or ridden with tension. We can't quite kick the addiction. Our child is still not physically well.

When the waiting begins to weigh you down, remember these Scriptures. And don't just remember them, say them out loud. There's power when you hear your own voice declare the Word of God. We don't know what tomorrow will bring, but we know God's Word will never fade away.

God is always with us, giving us Captain Marvel style power punches.

Day 2

REVIEW

If you are reading along in *The Fight to Flourish*, review chapters 16 and 17.

REMEMBER

> "When you're losing heart, when you feel like giving up, when the season you're in doesn't make sense, just wait. There's more. When it seems you're losing the fight, breathe, towel off, hydrate, lean in, and learn all you can. Keep fighting. Keep giving it all you've got. God promises that there is more." (*The Fight to Flourish*, page 222)

REFLECT

Write down what you have learned, a breakthrough you experienced, or a shift in perspective from this video session or discussion.

_____

_____

_____

What Scripture spoke to you most this week? Try to memorize it. Write it down below and then put it on an index card or sticky note and place it wherever you spend some alone time each day (the bathroom, your car, on a kitchen window or laptop cover).

_____

_____

_____

_____

There's no pushing past

the growth of a seed.

You just have to wait.

Day 3

STUDY

Read 2 Corinthians 4:16–18:

> "Therefore we do not lose heart. Even though our outward man is perishing, yet the inward man is being renewed day by day. For our light affliction, which is but for a moment, is working for us a far more exceeding and eternal weight of glory, while we do not look at the things which are seen, but at the things which are not seen. For the things which are seen are temporary, but the things which are not seen are eternal."

When we focus on Jesus, we don't give up all our attention to what is happening right now—on the load we are carrying, on the pressure that is weighing us down, on the problem we cannot solve. When we focus on Jesus, we see our difficulties as the temporary pain that will lead to forever wholeness and healing.

Write down how the above Scripture encourages you in whatever challenge you are currently facing.

_____

_____

_____

_____

When you think about the future, what do you most think about? Do you have a hard time thinking about God's kingdom and all that awaits you in eternity? What might it look like to begin to wait for this day as a citizen of heaven still living on this earth?

_____

_____

_____

_____

Paul wrote in Colossians 3:1–4,

> "If then you were raised with Christ, seek those things which are above, where Christ is, sitting at the right hand of God. Set your mind on things above, not on things on the earth. For you died, and your life is hidden with Christ in God. When Christ *who is* our life appears, then you also will appear with Him in glory."

Proverbs 23:18 tells us,

> "For surely there is a hereafter, and your hope will not be cut off."

REFLECT

As believers, our faith informs our worldview. We see things differently than others. Our outlook on earthly life is hopeful because we have received the gift of eternal life. This is not our home. Our real forever home is with Jesus where we will live for all eternity.

Still, the reality of heaven doesn't negate the fact that life is hard, and sometimes it hurts. We face trouble here and now.

Living with an eternal mindset is more practical than you may think. When we shift our thinking into this gear, it helps us encourage ourselves, build one another up, and change our perspective on suffering and hardship.

Think about these three keys. Under each one, write down one or two specific ways your life can illustrate that key. (I.e., "encourage ourselves"—I can face the future knowing that Jesus is already there.)

◆ Encourage ourselves

_____

_____

_____

◆ Build one another up

_____

_____

_____

◆ Change our perspective on suffering and hardship

_____

_____

_____

We are not fighting

forward alone. God

is in our corner.

Day 4

REMEMBER

"God loves you. He cares for you. He is with you. He will fight for you. Your part? Believe Him. Trust Him. Keep your hands up in surrender, and just keep walking. When you come up against the impossible, when you feel like you're losing the fight, when you're so weary you can't lift your fists to protect yourself, look up. See that God is there, and watch Him fight for you." (*The Fight to Flourish*, page 236)

MOVE FORWARD

As you complete this study, think about and write down three ways this teaching has informed your faith and encouraged you to lean into God, knowing it is only through Him that you will grow, bloom and flourish.

1. _____

   _____

2. _____

   _____

3. _____

   _____

JENNIE'S PRAYER FOR YOU

Father, life can be so hard. But it can also be so wonderful. Help this beautiful soul to catch a glimpse of the glory in the trial, because it can be difficult to recognize it on our own. I pray that if she's tired or discouraged, You would surround her with Your love and Your grace. Give her the strength to keep showing up because there's so much in store for her around the corner. Create in her a mindset that is focused on eternity, because as bad as things get or feel in this place, You have prepared for her a forever home, a place where everything will finally be made right. Remind her that You have not left her alone, and that You will fight for her. In Jesus' name, I pray, amen.

A NOTE OF THANKS

I wanted to take this page and thank every person who worked on this curriculum. AJ, you worked your magic (again), and I'm so thankful for you. Sara, you are a beautiful person, and this curriculum is wonderful! Thank you for working so hard and putting your heart into this to make it beautiful. I'm so thankful God so sweetly surprised us both ;) and I haven't forgotten about our coffee date.

The W team and Harper team :: Thank you for helping me and rolling with my out-of-the box requests.

Marshall and Daniel and Nate and all the Process Creative team :: Thank you for making it so easy to film and do something that was so hard for me.

Levi :: Your advice and help and concern and care floors me. I couldn't have done any of this without you!

Thank you Autumn, Emily, Esther, and my incredible Fresh Life team, who helped me in the filming process :: What a joy to work with you!

And to everyone I missed :: Thank you for helping me fight to flourish; I'm so thankful for you!

BIBLE STUDY
SOURCE
for women

powered by ChurchSource

Connecting you with the best in

BIBLE STUDY RESOURCES

from many of the world's

MOST TRUSTED BIBLE TEACHERS

| JESS CONNOLLY | JENNIE ALLEN | JADA EDWARDS | JENNIE LUSKO |

Providing

WOMEN'S MINISTRY AND
SMALL GROUP LEADERS

with the **INSPIRATION, ENCOURAGEMENT, AND RESOURCES** to grow your ministry

powered by ChurchSource

join our
COMMUNITY

Use our BIBLE STUDY FINDER to quickly find the perfect study for your group, learn more about all the new studies available, and download FREE printables to help you make the most of your Bible study experience.

BibleStudySourceForWomen.com

FIND THE *perfect* BIBLE STUDY
for you and your group in 5 MINUTES or LESS!

Find the right study for your women's group
by answering four easy questions:

1. WHAT TYPE OF STUDY DO YOU WANT TO DO?

- *Book of the Bible:* Dive deep into the study of a Bible character, or go through a complete book of the Bible systematically, or add tools to your Bible study methods toolkit.

- *Topical Issues:* Have a need in a specific area of life? Study the Scriptures that pertain to that need. Topics include prayer, joy, purpose, balance, identity in Christ, and more.

2. WHAT LEVEL OF TIME COMMITMENT BETWEEN SESSIONS WOULD YOU LIKE?

- *None:* No personal homework
- *Minimal:* Less than 30 minutes of homework
- *Moderate:* 30 minutes to one hour of homework
- *Substantial:* An hour or more of homework

3. WHAT IS YOUR GROUP'S BIBLE KNOWLEDGE?

- *Beginner:* Group is comprised mostly of women who are new to the Bible or who don't feel confident in their Bible knowledge.

- *Intermediate:* Group has some experience with studying the Bible, and they have some familiarity with the stories in the Bible.

- *Advanced:* Group is comfortable with the Bible, and can handle the challenge of searching the Scriptures for themselves.

4. WHAT FORMAT DO YOU PREFER?

- *Print and Video:* Watch a Bible teacher on video, followed by a facilitated discussion.

- *Print Only:* Have the group leader give a short talk and lead a discussion of a study guide or a book.

Get Started!
Plug your answers into the **Bible Study Finder**, and discover the studies that best fit your group!

Check out the Bible Study Finder at:
BibleStudySourceForWomen.com

Also available from Levi Lusko

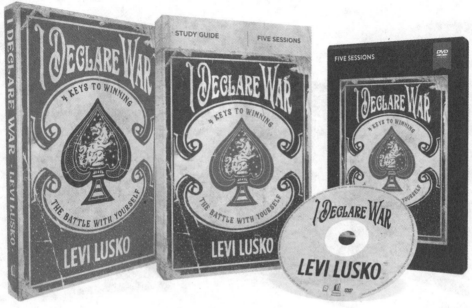

Book
9780785220862

Study Guide
9780310094876

DVD
9780310094913

In *I Declare War*, Levi candidly shares about his struggles with moodiness, bullying, suicidal thoughts, night terrors, and difficulty managing himself. He identifies four weapons you have at your disposal—thoughts, words, behaviors, and power—and illustrates how to use them to achieve ongoing victory.

In the five-session study, Levi helps you apply the principles in *I Declare War* to your life. The study guide includes video notes, group discussion questions, and personal study and reflection materials for in-between sessions.

Available now at your favorite bookstore,
or streaming video on StudyGateway.com.